A Mother on Her Sick Child in 1931

Sylvia Cohn

A Mother on Her Sick Child in 1931

Her Words for Us Today

Title photo: Esther Cohn on her first birthday

The Publishers:
Alfried Kohlschütter had a long career as Professor of Pediatrics in the University of Hamburg.
Brigitte Kohlschütter, M.D., practiced anesthesiology and internal medicine in University Medical Centers in Switzerland and Germany.

The Translator:
Elinore Chapman Herschkowitz is a writer and former teacher. She grew up in the United States and lives in Switzerland.

Typesetting and layout:
Johannes Kohlschütter, Freiburg, using Adobe InDesign.
Set in Neue Helvetica and Minion Pro fonts.

Printing and distribution on behalf of the publishers:
tredition GmbH, Halenreie 40-44, 22359 Hamburg

ISBN: 978-3-347-66855-3

To the Reader

An anxious mother writes about the diseases of her 4-year-old daughter in the 1930s. Countless parents have suffered similarly terrifying episodes, artists have portrayed their pain. We are familiar with these situations and feel we know them as a fact. Why then do these mother's notes deserve our special attention?

An intelligent woman observes her beloved child with amazing accuracy. Within the short period of nine months the little girl, Esther, is afflicted with three classical infectious diseases one after the other without interruption, diseases which in our rich world of today are practically unknown. By "we" we include doctors as well as parents. When we think of "childhood diseases" we understand diseases that we think of as harmless, in the worst case unpleasant, diseases, for example, measles (a disease that can, however, lead to death or permanent brain damage). We must keep in mind that under other circumstances these "forgotten" diseases, these terrors of the past, could possibly return. And when we take a broader view over the scourge of infectious disease we see that the burden of a seriously ill child is often not only a question of its survival. The question arises of whether the child will grow up and be able to live on their own later without the constant support of loving parents.

In the case of little Esther her development over the course of many months of pain and despair seems to have taken a rather favorable direction. To be sure, an accidental lapse in hospital procedure brings about a temporary catastrophe, but the child's constitution, together with great efforts on the part of the medical staff and competent nursing care, leads to her survival and partial rehabilitation. In spite of some remaining paralysis of her arms and legs, the child learns to walk following a long period of training with the support of her mother and with the use of proper training equipment. From other sources we know that the the poor little soul who had to bear so much went on to become an intelligent pupil. Her own diary also shows evidence of this.

Unfortunately, this story of suffering and the brave efforts to overcome it has a dreadful ending for its heroes: The child, her mother and her doctor in the Children's Hospital all died a violent death during the years 1939–1944 – because they were Jews.

Alfried Kohlschütter, 2022

Esther-Lore Cohn was born on September 18th, 1926, as the first child of her mother. When she was 13 months old her mother began to write a diary that describes the girl's favorable development until the age of 3 ½ years. Then begin the anxious times reported in the following copy of a page from Sylvia's diary.

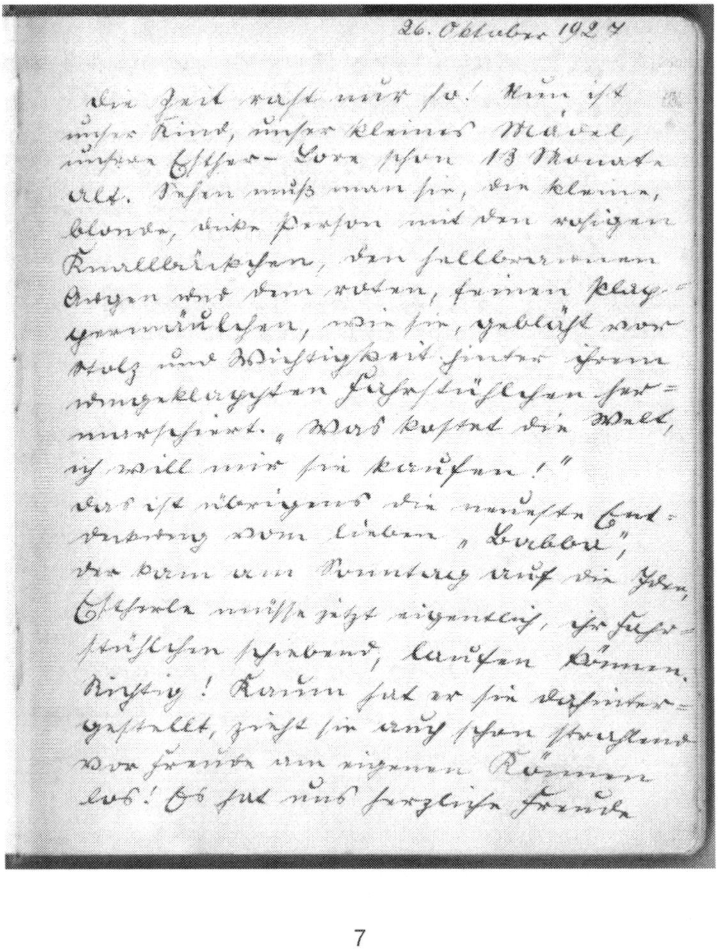

26. Oktober 1927

Die Zeit rast nur so! Nun ist
unser Kind, unser kleines Mädel,
unsere Esther-Lore schon 13 Monate
alt. Sehen muß man sie, die kleine,
blonde, dicke Person mit den rosigen
Knallbäckchen, den hellbraunen
Augen und dem roten, feinen Plap-
permäulchen, wie sie, gebläht vor
Stolz und Wichtigkeit hinter ihrem
umgeklappten Fahrstühlchen her=
marschiert. „Was kostet die Welt,
ich will mir sie kaufen!"
Das ist übrigens die neueste Ent-
deckung vom lieben „Bubbe",
der kam am Sonntag auf die Idee,
Estherle müsste jetzt eigentlich, ihr Fahrstühlchen schiebend, laufen können.
Richtig! Kaum hat er sie dahinter=
gestellt, zieht sie auch schon strahlend
vor Freude am eigenen Können
los! Es hat uns herzliche Freude

January 1930. Esther with her younger sister Myriam

From the Diary of Sylvia Cohn

For Fastnacht[1] I turned Estherlein[2] into a cute children's nurse. Sewed everything myself, decorated the dolls' baby carriage to look neat and attractive. The child looked irresistibly pretty and special. Everybody, and by that I mean really EVERYBODY, stopped to admire my little daughter.

Esther dressed up as a children's nurse

Early June 1930

After that it was not a good time for any of us. On April 7th Mutterle[3] had to go to the hospital in Gengenbach for a very serious operation. She didn't want to go, and she was a regular scaredy-cat about it. But in spite of the pain and many a diffi-

[1]Carneval, a mainly Catholic spring festival before the beginning of the 40 days of fasting (no meat) before Easter. The parade in this year was on Tuesday, March 4th, 1930.
[2]Estherlein: Diminutive of Esther, little Esther
[3]Diminutive of Mummy, the writer herself

cult hour during the first days after the operation, with God's help all went well. My recuperation took place normally and without any complications in less than 4 weeks.

Naturally, Esther could visit her Mutti[4] often in Gengenbach once the first post-operative days were over. But very soon I noticed that the mild cough that she had had already before I left had become gradually worse, and I was worried because I didn't trust Aunt Hilda's (who took my place at home) opinion that it was a common cold.

Alas, my fears were realized all too soon. All the typical signs of whooping cough[5] appeared, and Dr. Bloch soon confirmed this diagnosis. When I came home from the hospital the beginning of May, still fairly weak and in need of rest, the child was, of course, in the period during which the disease gathers strength, and her suffering was intense, particularly during the night. The coughing attacks became more frequent and so severe that the already anxious child became terrified when she sensed the approach of an impending attack, and her screaming brought on the attack in full force. It was a real torture to be standing by in "Emergency Mode" without being able to help and having to watch how the child coughed and wheezed and had to vomit and how comparatively long such a fit lasted! As I said before, it was worst at night!

And since Mother was back home again, she naturally had to get up many times in the night to be with her child. There were 15–17 attacks per night at the peak of the disease. The

[4]Mummy

[5]Whooping cough (pertussis) is a highly contagious disease of the respiratory tract caused by a bacterial infection and characterized by coughing fits, with a predicted course of several weeks. It typically starts like a common cold, followed by a high-pitched intake of breath that sounds like a "whoop" and eventually subsides after many weeks. It is a serious disease that can be lethal in young infants. At the time of this story an effective vaccine was just being developed.

child looked miserable. And I, the Mutti, was understandably miserable, too, because I was still recovering from my operation and needed rest. Instead, I had a sick child and sleepless nights. – To all this, poor little sister Myriam had meanwhile also contracted the disease and heartily joined in the coughing and "whooping". Dr. Bloch[6] gave both the children injections with whooping cough vaccine, but at first this brought no relief. So he recommended as the best therapy an immediate change of air[7]. Now this was not exactly easy financially at this time[8]. However, our dear Vati[9] decided to send us away without delay, to the great benefit of all involved.

Now the first task was to find a suitable person to accompany us. With my awkward and grumbling Else the undertaking would have been absolutely impossible, and I was still too weak myself for the strenuous care of the two sick children. The choice fell on the young nurse, Hilde Westenfelder, and this turned out to be a good one. She was a cautious, diligent and pleasant girl, with whom I was in good hands in every way. – So everything was packed up in haste, and Vati brought us to Ühlingen in the Black Forest, a village set in a charming location surrounded by wooded areas at an altitude of 650 meters. There we took up our quarters at the Posthorn Inn (a customer of ours)[10]. We were provided with beautiful, airy rooms, good food and everything we needed. To be sure, it was raining hard upon our arrival, but according to the in-

[6]Dr. Werner Bloch, the family's young pediatrician in Offenburg (See Epilogue)

[7]A "change of air" was a frequent doctor's advice because psychological factors seem to contribute to the perpetuation of symptoms.

[8]In 1929 as the Wall Street Crash led to a worldwide depression, Germany suffered particularly hard as a result of the recall of US loans, which caused its economy to collapse. Unemployment skyrocketed, and many families lost their savings.

[9]Affectionate name for „Father"

[10]The family had a wine business in Offenburg.

structions of Dr. Bloch the children were to be taken out for walks in any weather, even when it was raining, and this did them good, particularly little Esther. Already during the first night her coughing fits decreased from 14 to 12.

However, Myriam's whooping cough symptoms increased rapidly and with unexpected force. The child also had many utterly terrifying coughing fits. She got very pale for minutes at a time and even seemed about to faint. But, since the little rascal is less nervous and on the whole calmer than her sister, she overcame the severity of the attacks better than Esther did. As the series of injections had to be completed, we looked up the local doctor, Uncle Doctor Florack, who then treated the children during the whole time of their stay. I got to know him as an admirable person and competent doctor, and our relationship soon took a turn from the professional to the more purely "personal", so that I see him today as a friend, whose acquaintance I would no longer want to miss. –

Now, after the rainy weather, there followed also sunny days, and my little children and I took full advantage of them, with diligent walking tours and time spent in the forest rich in ozone[11]. Esther's symptoms decreased visibly, and her appetite improved, – I, too, recovered well. Only the little one suffered badly, but it would have surely been just as bad if not worse at home. And the stay in Ühlingen helped her, too, at least to overcome the peak of her whooping cough faster. So the Black Forest helped us all, and after 2½ weeks we returned home more or less recovered. To be sure, both children coughed and whooped for another 1–2 months, but it was no longer so bad, more like a gradual fading away!

[11] A typical (today outdated) claim of the tourist branch at that time

The Posthorn Inn in Ühlingen. On left: Esther on the front stairs. On right: “Ring-around-the-Rosie”, with cousins Walter and Hans

Picking wild orchids[12]

December 1930

I don't have anything more to relate that was good in this year. My heart always bleeds when I think of it, – and that is almost always – and you will find it understandable after I have described it all that my hand and pen have refused for so long to continue my chronicles as I know I should. –

After my little Esther had happily recovered from her whooping cough she was a somewhat delicate child, like before, but she was full of life, content and full of fun.

[12] Now forbidden because wild orchids are protected by environmental laws

But it was actually for only about 3–4 weeks that she could enjoy her life as a happy, normal child. From this time, it was in July, we have many nice memories of how Vati drove us, little Esther and me, in the car to the beach, how on hot days we made ourselves at home there for whole afternoons, how proud little Esther marched around in her pretty blue bathing suit, and how the little rascal was sure to be found where young men and ladies were playing ball! And the independent little imp was also good for bringing back "Snails" (cinnamon buns), in spite of the fact that the Bath House, where snacks were sold was a long stretch from the beach where we were installed. She even always brought back the exact number of buns and the correct change! For this, Vati was particularly proud of his 3 ½-year-old daughter! –

Soon, however, these pleasures turned to vinegar, because Esther Child had to stay in bed with fever and a sore throat. She had, as often before, swollen tonsils, and I treated her with gargling and throat compresses. After about 8 days she was healthy again and could get up. At this time Aunt Gretel was there with Rudi and little Hans, and during this time the children were often together, sometimes to play, sometimes to go for walks. And they all enjoyed this. A very nice, but unfortunately the last beautiful memory for a long time was the excursion we made together to Lahr by the Hohbergsee, on which Aunt U., Amin, Gretel, Hans and little Rudi, as well as Flora, Ida, Vati, little Esther and I participated. It was a beautiful, cosy afternoon, the children enjoyed the see-saw and games, the grown-ups coffee and cake. In the evening, when we got home, everything was in perfect order. The next day little Esther had a high fever. It began with 38.6°[13] and climbed rapidly to 40°, so that I was deadly alarmed.

Dr. Bloch, who was rapidly called to the scene, made the diagnosis of a new throat infection[14] with redness and swelling of the tonsils, which we treated accordingly. However, it was strange, that in spite of careful administrations (one did what one could) there was no improvement, even after several days. The fever remained constantly quite high, her throat didn't get better, swallowing was extraordinarily painful, the child's behavior was odd, and she was very impatient. The nights were terrible. Esterlein couldn't sleep in spite of being given all possible medications. She was apparently in pain and screamed constantly, so that Rösle, the girl who took care of her, and I could never get to bed.

In the mornings the child was tired and listless and slept until noon. Meanwhile her fever was constantly high, and I lived in dreadful fear. After 5–6 days the glands behind her ears were slightly swollen. The swelling increased rapidly, the fever climbed further, and the child was in terrible pain. Now the situation was almost unbearable, and we could hardly help. The warm chamomile compresses and the hot oil wraps over the glands brought little relief. – A urine test showed traces of protein, so that we lived in truly deadly fear[15]. –

[13] 38.6° = 101.5 F, 40° = 104 F

[14] Pharyngitis, a sore throat, is one of the most frequent and most of the time harmless children's diseases. It is usually caused by a viral infection, does not respond to antibiotics and resolves on its own. In Esther, however, it was caused by bacteria. Before the era of antibiotics such an infection could lead to severe complications, in this case to suppuration (pus) breaking its way to the outside of the neck.

[15] An elevated protein content in the urine raises the suspicion that the child's sore throat was caused by bacteria of the type A streptococci. Such infections can trigger off violent immune reactions in the body that lead to severe damage of the heart and kidneys. While an initial streptococcal infection is easily treatable by antibiotics today, the late organ damage is ominous and does not respond to medication.

On the eleventh day a sample was taken of a strange, white coating of the throat lining and analyzed by Dr. Bloch, who thought it might be diphtheria[16]. At this news we decided with great fear to send little Esther Child away immediately, also because of the danger that Myriam might contract the disease, and take her to the famous Children's Hospital of Prof. Lust in Karlsruhe[17], whom Dr. Bloch had particularly recommended to us. With extreme haste (There was no time to lose.) we packed the most necessary items and drove with Dr. Bloch in the car as fast as possible to Karlsruhe, poor little Esther with 40° fever on my lap.

January 6th, 1931

When we arrived the Professor was away. This was not a problem, because the very experienced assistant medical director, Dr. Courtin, who had been at the clinic for a long time, was there and examined the child immediately and thoroughly. He made no definite promises, however, because he made the exact diagnosis dependent on the result of a more recent smear and from the blood test – but he didn't think for the moment of diphtheria, rather of a severe angina. The little imp was tucked into bed (She had a very pretty private room.), and in the evening we traveled home. However, I promised Estherlein that I would visit her in Karlsruhe already the next day. It

[16] Diphtheria: in the past called "the children's strangling angel", is a serious infection of the upper airways, caused by bacteria that can secrete a toxin that damages the heart and other organs. The disease can be prevented by vaccination. The first vaccine was developed in 1924 and approved for use in Germany in 1936.

[17] Professor Franz Lust, Medical Director of the Urban Children's Hospital Karlsruhe (see Epilogue)

The Pension Victoria in Karlsruhe in 1908, later the main building of the Franz-Lust-Children's Hospital in Karlsruhe

Doctor Bloch, Nazi Refugee, Locates Here

1937

DR. WERNER H. BLOCH

On left: Dr. Werner Bloch, Pediatrician in Offenburg. Newspaper clipping USA 1937. On right: Franz Lust, Medical Director of the Urban Children's Hospital Karlsruhe

was a Sunday. Of course, I then went there, and Vati too. We were both very worried and feared the worst.

Also on Sunday one couldn't give us any definite result, but on Monday the Professor came home, and by Tuesday the Heidelberg lab had the results of the lab tests, – so that they could tell me on Tuesday with certainty that Estherlein had <u>no</u> "diphtherit"[18], but rather severe angina with infection and swelling of the lymph glands.

This came as a relief to us at the moment, in contrast to our fears. Estherle[19] always greeted my arrival with great joy, but she got terribly upset when I took my leave. She cried, screamed and behaved in such a manner that after the first week the Professor explained that he would prefer that in the interest of the child I would not come so often. I should give Estherlein time to get used to her situation. This we did. When I did return, Estherle had already become fully accustomed to her new hospital routine.

But how did the little rascal look! Her whole little head, hair, throat, everything was bandaged up. Only her tiny face peeked out and that had become quite thin from the constant fever of the past weeks! – She got warm antiphlogistine[20] compresses

[18] "Diphtherit": another word for diphtheria, from the French "diphtherite", that comes from the Greek word diphthera ("two pieces of leather"). In a typical case one may see two dark, membrane-like areas of tissue in the throat of a patient.

[19] Estherle: Diminutive of "Esther"

[20] Antiphlogistine is a medicated poultice dressing for painful parts of the body. It was popular during the early part of the twentieth century. The compress contained glycerin, boric acid, salicylic acid, methyl salicylate, peppermint oil, eucalyptus oil, and a kind of porcelain clay. These ingredients were stirred together to a thick warm paste that was applied to painful places on the body. In the case of infections that tended to the formation of abcesses it was believed that that the procedure would stimulate the so called "maturation" of a blister that contained pus – which one could then release by cutting the blister.

over her glands. These were a mixture made with a kind of therapeutic clay that should either reduce the swelling of the glands or open them if they contained pus. Her tonsils were treated by gargling with potassium permanganate[21]. This treatment was continued in Karlsruhe for 4 weeks, during which time Estherle still ran a rather high fever, which was evidence that something was brewing on the side of the glands. By the end of the fourth week the "edematous" swelling of the glands had been reduced due to the application of the therapeutic clay to the point where one could pinpoint the location of the source of the pus.

When my husband and I came by chance to Karlsruhe on a Saturday, we were told at the clinic that they had called us in Offenburg in the meantime to tell us that the child would need an immediate operation on her neck[22].

We quickly went up to the child, who was unaware of the coming procedure and playing in her bed and who was very happy to see us. At this moment I was equally shocked and glad to see this lack of fearful anticipation in such a child because I secretly compared this with the fear and awful torment of an adult who knows that they face a serious operation. – How blessed is an innocent child compared to this!

Already after a quarter of an hour they took the child away to the operation theater. She cried a bit, but only from fear of the unfamiliar, what they intended, and because they were taking her away from us. –

[21] Potassium permanganate is a chemical compound that was introduced as a disinfectant in the 19th century. It has been widely used to treat a variety of infectious skin conditions.

[22] The throat infection was obviously caused by bacteria and had initiated a suppurating process that eventually led to the formation of abscesses (painful collections of pus) under the skin of the neck. These abscesses had to be cut open.

We, my dear husband and I, now spent an anxious, anxious hour. Fear and pity for our child tied up our throats. Finally they brought the little bundle back to us. The surgical nurse carried her in her arms and laid her in her bed. She was still sleeping, unconscious due to the etherization[23]. However, she soon opened her eyes and broke out in an absolutely terrifying, scream that shook us to the core and took our breath away. However, the Professor assured us that this was no sign of pain but rather the typical result of the etherization and that she was still not yet conscious.

We didn't quite believe him. – He also told us that the approximately 3-cm-long[24] incision on the left side of her neck had brought good results, for a large amount of thin liquid pus had flowed out[25]. And he believed that it would get better from now on. He added that he wanted us now to go out to eat and not stay there until Little Esther gained full consciousness but rather reappear only in the afternoon. We obeyed him and slipped out with a heavy heart..

It is understandable that neither of us had any appetite for food that day, and the waiter at Moninger's could take away almost as much as he had brought. –

When we returned to the clinic after lunch, around 3 o'clock, we expected, especially me, in fear and trepidation, to find a

[23]Etherization is a method of anaesthetization by inhalation of ether fumes. Ether was introduced for the use as an anesthetic in Boston in 1846 and was used for this purpose for over one hundred years. Etherized patients are unconscious and do not feel pain but continue to breathe. Unwanted effects such as distorted thinking and hallucinations can occur. Today anesthesiologists combine different ingredients to induce sleep, overcome pain and to relax muscles, thus avoiding an ether overdose.

[24]About 1.2 inches

[25]A Latin medical saying goes: "Ubi pus ibi evacua"—Where you find pus, let it out! This is based on the experience that cutting an abscess (a pus-filled blister) will not only reduce local pain but will also sometimes lead to a surprising change for the better in the whole patient, as in the example of this little girl.

whiny, feverous child tormented by pain. Who can describe my astonishment when I cautiously tiptoe into the room and see – a laughing, happy, glowing Esther Child sitting up in bed, playing and glad to see her parents come. I was completely astounded. The child had no pain (for the first time in weeks). This was because the mean pus that had caused the tension in her throat had been expelled. She had no memory of what had happened – and for the first time in weeks she had no fever! I was overjoyed about the unexpectedly good result of the operation – and we drove home in the evening with a lighter heart than usual. For everything was headed in the right direction! –

The wound had to be kept open for a few days, about 8 days, so that the pus could drain. The good child had had no more fever since the day of the incision, and we were looking forward to taking her home in the near future.

When we visited her on September 18th, her birthday, on which she turned 4, she was very pleased with the many pretty things that I brought her. She was in good spirits and felt well, and we invited the nurses to her room for coffee and cake so that the Little One could have her party like last year at home. This was also the day on which she was allowed to get up for the first time, to be sure, somewhat miserable and still weak on her legs, but at least – she could do it! All in all it was a beautiful, if rather exciting day, for the Little One. Our hearts rejoiced at being able to promise Estherlein on parting that we would bring her home in 8 days, on the day after Rosch Haschana[26]. – Everything was in order, and we were happy and grateful to have come so far again. – Things would take a different turn.

[26] Jewish New Year celebration

March 18th, 1931

With all my might I want to force myself now to finish writing my sad report before the time of my confinement[27]. Then whether this book will otherwise ever be completed, – that one doesn't yet know today. –

So, we spent September 18th with our child and left her with a good feeling. Then on September 19th they told us on the telephone that Estherlein was complaining of a severe headache, on September 20th they gave me the news that the child now had a fever in addition to her headache, – they couldn't yet determine what it was coming from. --On Sunday, September 21st I called early in the morning, nothing had changed yet. However, Nurse Ilse brought Estherlein, who was homesick, to the telephone. –When I heard the bright, dear little voice call "Mutti, dear Mutti, come right to me!", I immediately promised the poor little heart to come to her with the next train, – -and that's just what I did!

But I didn't like the looks of my child on this Sunday. – The Professor was away, His chief medical assistant wasn't sure yet what to do about the onset of the new fever that continued and was accompanied by headache and a stiff neck[28].

Estherle was hot, her little heart beat fiercely, and she acted strange and restless and wanted to eat lying down instead of sitting up. And the food made her reject it, so that she vomited it out afterwards. –

On this evening I traveled home, sad and full of new worry, without knowing what was wrong with my child. – I had seen

[27] Eva was born on March 27th, 1931.

[28] The mother describes here the onset of the ominous disease of meningitis. This begins with headache and a painful neck stiffness caused by an irritation of the meninges, the membranes that protect the brain and spinal cord.

enough and knew that my child was again sick. When I was picked up that evening at the station in Offenburg I said right away to my dear husband: "Ed, I don't like the looks of that child!" –

The next day (Monday) I called again. In the meantime Professor Lust had returned. Right away he already had his suspicions, which he only communicated to me indistinctly because he could only tell me the exact diagnosis after the chemical blood test was over. – He spoke of a "nerve infection". And in the meantime her little left arm was showing signs of paralysis. – There, now we had our Rosch Haschana!

Dr. Bloch was immediately summoned and explained to us what this could possibly mean: "Poliomyelitis[29]". Oh, horrible shock! I am not capable, even by way of a hint, to say what anguish I, we, suffered through! –

Tuesday evening brought terrible certainty! In addition to the left arm, the right arm was also afflicted by paralysis. The Professor no longer doubted the fact. The blood test had confirmed his suspicion, – Estherlein, my golden Estherlein was afflicted by spinal polio. The gruesome demon of this spring and summer, at the thought of which the heart of every mother stands still, the terrible strangler of healthy happy childhood beauty, – had wrapped his paws around our poor little darling!

[29]Poliomyelitis (inflammation of the grey matter in the spinal cord), or "infantile paralysis, is an infectious disease of the nervous system caused by the polio virus. The disease first affects the meninges, producing headache and neck stiffness and later on reaches, to varying degrees, nerve cells of the spinal cord. Frequent and dreaded consequences are permanent paralyses of various body parts, even of the whole body, including the respiratory system. The development of polio vaccines (the first using the inactivated poliovirus and delivered as an injection, and a second using a weakened polio virus and given orally) are among the great achievements of medicine.

My God, we didn't know what we should plead for, pray for, in those hours: the child's death or her life! On Wednesday, the second day of Rosch Haschana, my dear husband and I set off on our sad trip to Karlsruhe to see our poor little child again. – First we were taken to the Professor, who wanted to speak to us. He spoke in the sense that in spite of everything one could be lucky if the paralysis stayed in the arms and didn't spread to the legs as well. The child was, of course, still hovering in an acute worsening stage of the disease and therefore still in an absolutely life-threatening situation.

He answered our reproachful and bitter questions about the why and wherefore of this misfortune, after the child had already fully recovered and was free of fever, by shrugging his shoulders. One could never know. I could have brought her this infectious bacillus[30] as well as anybody else of her visitors. That the doctors or the nurses could have been the source of infection, which is our unshakeable opinion, was a possibility to which he wouldn't admit. In spite of this, it is the most likely possibility, for without the knowledge of our Professor[31] there were about 15 other cases of spinal polio in the hospital. They were housed in a separate part of the building, but the doctors who were treating them were the same as those in the rest of the hospital. Is it not the most likely conclusion that the child caught her infection from them? Then that she already carried the germ in her from Offenburg, according to another theory of the Professor, is a possibility I can exclude, because Estherle had already spent 5 weeks in Karlsruhe before the disease appeared and the spinal bacillus only lives 8–10 in

[30] The word "bacillus" is incorrect. Polio is caused by a virus. However, lay persons sometimes used the word bacillus in the more general sense of "infectious agent" or "germ".

[31] This was most likely ironic, since it is hard to believe that the Professor was unaware of the situation in his hospital.

the body before the disease breaks out. – There is the contradiction right there! But what help was our indignation and rebellion now over whether the cause was this or that? The disease remained the same, our Esther Child was lying there miserable and fatally ill. –

When we visited her in her new station where she was now, we found a whimpering, miserable looking, pale yellow child, who sometimes screamed raucously in unnatural high piping tones[32], particularly when she was attacked by the horrible back pains that are the typical symptom of this disease. Indeed, it is an inflammation of the nerves in the spinal cord and all the nerves going out from it. The further the inflammation progresses, the more paralyses appear. It was dreadful. – As a last attempt to limit the paralyses, the Professor wanted to make a transfusion from a child who had already recovered from the disease and was healthy again[33]. Of course, the blood for the transfusion had first to be chemically prepared, and that lasts at least 24 hours.

Then, in spite of all our cares and even anger at the hospital, it was touching to see how impatiently and desperately the Professor raced from the sick bed of our Darling to the preparation of the blood serum, whether it was not yet ready, – and back again. Ten times a day the man came over from the main building to our child to see how she was doing. And even if he, or let's say "his system", did bear a certain guilt for this whole

[32] Also referred to as a "cerebral cry"

[33] This was an experimental attempt to use blood from convalescent poliomyelitis patients for the passive immunization of a patient with the ongoing disease in order to prevent further damage to the nerve cells. For a city hospital at that time this was a formidable procedure and required taking blood from the donor patient (here, a child), preparing the antibody-containing fraction of the blood in the laboratory and infusing it into the veins of the girl, with many precautions to be taken. The principle of this treatment for a dangerous viral infection has seen its rebirth in the present era of the COVID-19 pandemic.

misfortune, we still have to admit that the man called up every possible means of relief, all that science could offer, all that empathy, human kindness and competent nursing care could do, in order to save our child for us. – And he did save her. Even if she wasn't as she was before. However, that did not lie in his power!

We drove home on this evening with heavy hearts. – Early the next morning, on Thursday, we drove right back to Karlsruhe, and Dr. Bloch came with us. Ach, those were terrible hours! What sight was awaiting us? Had the disease let up over night? Or had it continued with its work of destruction? Frightening questions! They would soon be answered. We arrived and found – deadly serious faces – and a completely lamed Esther Child. Overnight, the awful progress of the disease.

Now both legs were paralyzed, the abdominal wall, too, as well as the bladder, the intestines. Only one step further – a tiny step, and her lungs will be affected, her breathing center – and her little heart will come to a stop. –

My God! What, what could we wish for, what could we hope for? Her breath was already rattling, short and weak. We all stood around her little bed. The Professor and his assistant doctors came and went. Then the moment came,--the blood transfusion was ready. Afterwards, like in the days before, a lumbal puncture. A needle is inserted into the spinal cord in order to remove some spinal fluid and reduce the pressure on the brain. This should bring about a relief of the pain. That was an anxious day! In spite of the transfusion the Professor expected the worst in the night. The disease had already progressed so far. And actually only a wonder can save our miserable Little One. –

An endless day! In the evening Dr. Bloch and my husband parted from me. I didn't let them convince me to go home, too. I stayed with my child. They put a narrow field bed into the room for me. The night, the night I feared, began. It was impossible to think of sleep. As long as the strong medications worked, the child had a bit of rest. When they were no longer effective the clear, high cry of pain began again. "Mutti[34], put me in another position! Mutti, put me in another position!"[35] Her whole body hurt. But this night passed, – and little Esther was still alive. Early in the morning a shattered and exhausted woman sneaked out of the hospital and into the nearby Hardt Forest, partly with pangs of bitterness, partly with a glad heart, – in order to refresh up her tear-stained red eyes in the coolness of the fall morning. – – – –

I don't want to go into too much detail. Bad, mournful hours and days went by one after the other. And I don't wish any mother the need to see lying before her her beloved, blooming, beautiful child rendered over night helpless, lonely, tormented by pain, ruined, – without being able to help her in spite of all her love and mother's will. For weeks she hovered between death and life. For, after the crisis of the paralysis had been favorably overcome, after we had the knowledge that our child would at least remain alive, (but not yet how!), that is 8–10 days following the onset of the disease, – a double-sided pneumonia broke out and threw the child back again to the border between life and death. This was caused by the fact that Estherle had a cough just at the onset of the paralysis. Because she was lame and couldn't sit, couldn't breathe normally,

[34] Mummy

[35] In this stage of poliomyelitis, the combination of the symptoms of meningitis (painful stiffening of the muscles of neck and spine) and the paralyses of the limbs lead to the inability to adopt a more tolerable body position.

couldn't cough any more, the phlegm around her lungs became so firm that she got this pneumonia! –

Thank God – she survived this crisis, too, and showed us by this what an immense energy and will to live were present in the weak child. How could she otherwise have been able to persevere, the poor child? But, she lives. Now it was important to arm ourselves with patience and to see what time and competent, expert care could salvage for our child. –

Now follow weeks and months during which almost nothing, only millimeter steps, could be seen in the way of improvement. At first, after weeks, the fever gradually disappeared, then the pain. Then she could feel when she had to empty her bladder and intestines, before that this happened involuntarily. – Then she slowly learned to make awkward, little movements with her little right hand. Then the shrill voice disappeared. Again and again weeks and months passed between all these steps. Slowly she began to tolerate the food offered to her. Gradually, with her lying in bed, I tried to cut out pages with paper dolls by letting her little hand guide the scissors with my help and my left hand holding the cardboard, and, behold, it worked! – Ach, what suffering and care for me and Vati, what will the future bring, what will stay forever? No answer, only patience and time. –

The nursing care is touching: In the morning pine-needle baths, then massage, then electric stimulation[36], noon nap on the terrace, even in winter, then again a salt bath[37] with gymnastics in the water, in short, every imaginable measure

[36]Electric stimulation. Electrical muscle stimulation uses electric impulses delivered through electrodes on the skin, causing muscles to contract. The procedure is used as a rehabilitation tool and performed by physiotherapists.

[37]The high salt content of the salt baths increases the specific gravity of the water, making certain physiotherapeutic exercises easier for persons with motor disabilities.

was taken! In November she learned, only after 9 weeks, to sit up again. Three weeks later she already learned to stand up and made the first awkward attempts to walk, with support under both arms. After that a long time has passed, we now write March. It lasted a long time, but now for a long time little Esther has been getting up every day, and thank God, she can walk on her own. She can help herself again a bit with

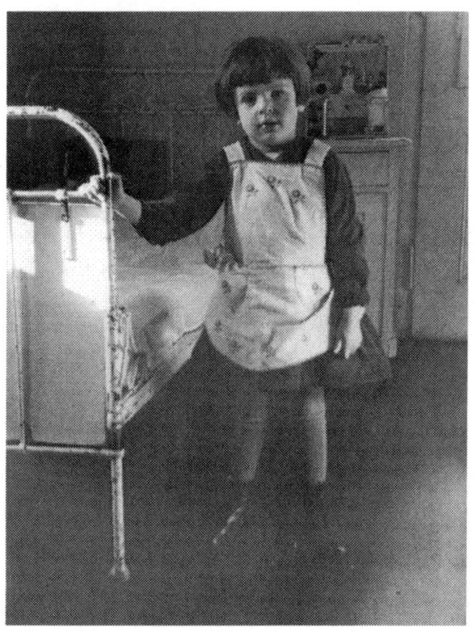

her little right hand. Her right upper arm is still quite weak – her left arm is unfortunately paralyzed. Will things get better? May God grant it. On May 1st we want to take our little darling home after an absence of three fourths of a year. At least she will now be a useful human being.

We have suffered and lived through a great deal of care, worry and heartbreak over you, my child. And the end is not in sight. I know. We will still have to go through a lot together, my Estherlein. One thing is certain, my Little One, as long as

I live I will help you to bear your sad fate in good spirits, to draw happiness from suffering, and – you shall never see, as long as you are little, how your mother's heart bleeds for you. I will educate you with a double amount of love, but also with double the demands on a child without handicap, so that I can make you capable of taking on your position in life as a whole person, because you will not always have parents to care for

you. And the help of strangers is rare and painful. – Therefore, you shall become independent, my darling, because your mother loves you very, very much. And so, for both of us –

Glück-auf![38]

***

[38] "Good luck!" Here as a frequent miner's greeting, instead of the more common expression "Viel Glück!"

Epilogue

The further fate of the main persons mentioned in the diary

The little girl, Esther Cohn, the main object of her mother's care in these notes: Because of her polio disability, when Esther reached school age, she was sent to the Children's Home of the Jewish Youth Aid, Antonienstrasse in Münich. This was an ambitious charitable institution. Since 1933 there were also many children living there who were waiting to be picked up by their parents who had already emigrated. Esther had a good time there in the beginning and got excellent grades in the school. In Bavaria she was not in danger of early deportation as were her mother and two sisters in Baden. However, the institution in Munich was dis-

Children's Home of the Jewish Youth Aid, Antonienstrasse 7 in Munich

solved step-wise. In July of 1942 Esther was deported to Theresienstadt, where she spent two years before October 16th, 1944, when she was taken with one of the last transports to Auschwitz and murdered there.

The mother, Sylvia Cohn, together with her daughter Myriam and her third daughter Eva, was seized completely unexpectedly as part of the so-called Wagner-Bürckel-Action on October 22, 1940 and deported from Offenburg to the concentration camp planned for Jews from Baden and the Saar Palatinate in Gurs, in Southern France. There she was able to give the two girls into the hands of strangers, whereby they survived. She herself was transported to Auschwitz on September 13th, 1942, where she was murdered. According to the official civil records she died on October 30th, 1942. The father had already been able to escape to England and make preparations for his family to join him there. However, these efforts turned out to be too late due to the unexpectedly early deportation in Baden.

The pediatrician Prof. Franz Lust was hired in 1920 as Medical Director of the newly established Karlsruhe Children's Hospital, located in the former Viktoria Pension. He was highly regarded in professional circles and generally popular. He was suspended as Clinic Director in 1933, after which time he practiced medicine in his apartment until the final prohibition of this professional activity. He was taken prisoner in the concentration camp Dachau following the "Reichskristallnacht" of November 9th, 1938. He planned to emigrate to the USA, but in view of his age of 59 years he didn't consider this a realistic professional perspective, and he committed suicide in 1939.

The pediatrician Dr. Werner Bloch in Offenburg had studied pediatrics under Prof. Lust. He was able with the help of relatives and friends to emigrate to the USA and at his young age he had no difficulty to put down roots, in both his personal relationships and professional life. He lived to the age of 93.

A Word of Thanks

Eva Mendelsson-Cohn, from Offenburg, the youngest sister of the girl mentioned in the diary, lives in England. In the course of her long life she has made great efforts to acquaint younger people with the story of the Jews in Germany since the 1930s. We thank her especially for entrusting us with a copy of the diary notes of her mother, Sylvia Cohn, and for the permission to use them for this publication.

Dr. Martin Ruch, publisher in Hesselhurst, has studied the fates of Jews in Baden for decades, particularly that of the Family Cohn in Offenburg, and has given them wide publicity in many books. We thank him for encouraging us to publish this work, for presenting us with a technically superior copy of the diary of Sylvia Cohn and for the biography of the pediatrician Dr. Werner Bloch in one of his books.

Ursula Flügler began early in her career as a high school teacher to introduce young people to the world of Jews in Offenburg. Her work brought her into contact with Eva Mendelsson-Cohn, which resulted in a lasting friendship. The publishers give special thanks to Ursula Flügler for calling our attention to the existence of Sylvia Cohn's diary.

Bibliography

Ruch, Martin: The Cohn Family. Diaries, Letters, Poems of a Jewish Family from Offenburg [Familie Cohn. Tagebücher, Briefe, Gedichte einer jüdischen Familie aus Offenburg]. Reiff, Offenburg 1992, ISBN-13: 978-3-922663-16-4 (out-of-print)

Ruch, Martin: “Meanwhile we have become star-studded”. The Diary of Esther Cohn (1926–1944) and the Children of the Antonian Institution in Munich [“Inzwischen sind wir nun besternt worden”. Das Tagebuch der Esther Cohn (1926–1944) und die Kinder vom Münchner Antonienheim]. KulturAgentur, Offenburg 2006, ISBN-13: 978-3-8334-5473-8

Ruch, Martin: Eva Mendelsson [in German]. seitenweise, Bühl 2018, ISBN-13: 978-3-943874-29-7

Ruch, Martin: Flight and Expulsion 1933–1945: Salvation abroad [Flucht und Vertreibung 1933–1945: Rettung in der Fremde]. Books on Demand, Norderstedt 2019, ISBN-13: 978-3-7494-9548-1

Sylvia Cohn (1904–1942): Poems and Letters. Martin Ruch and Eva Mendelsson (Editors), Translated by Marion Godfrey. Books on Demand, Norderstedt 2022, ISBN-13: 978-3-7557-9114-0

Credits for the Illustrations

Portrait of Prof. Lust: Rights owned by the Karlsruhe Children's Hospital. Image file from Karlsruhe Municipal Archive (11/DigA 8/9) accessed at https://stadtlexikon.karlsruhe.de/index.php?title=De:Lexikon:bio-0807&oldid=589928. Used with permission by the Karlsruhe Municipal Archive.

Photo of the Pension Victoria, Karlsruhe, around 1908, later Karlsruhe Children's Hospital: Printed in a special publication (Karlsruhe 1995, ISBN 3-88190-199-X). The picture is older than 100 years and no holder of the rights could be found (https://ka.stadtwiki.net/Datei:Victoria_Pensionat_1908.jpg).

Portrait Dr. Bloch: Newspaper article from the USA 1937, printed in "Flucht und Vertreibung 1933–1945" by Dr. Martin Ruch. Used with the author's permission.

Historic photo of the Posthorn Inn, Ühlingen in the Black Forest: Our thanks to Carina Frech for making it available to us.

Photo of the Children's Home of the Jewish Youth Aid in Munich: Ida-Seele-Archiv, 89407 Dillingen. Used with permission.

All other photos come from the diary of Sylvia Cohn.

Zeitfracht Medien GmbH
Ferdinand-Jühlke-Straße 7
99095 Erfurt, Deutschland
produktsicherheit@kolibri360.de